W●rk Readiness™

great
networking
skills

greg roza

ROSEN
PUBLISHING®
New York

Published in 2008 by The Rosen Publishing Group, Inc.
29 East 21st Street, New York, NY 10010

Copyright © 2008 by The Rosen Publishing Group, Inc.

First Edition

Library of Congress Cataloging-in-Publication Data

Roza, Greg.
Great networking skills / Greg Roza.—1st ed.
    p. cm.—(Work readiness)
Includes bibliographical references and index.
ISBN-13: 978-1-4042-1420-0 (library binding)
1. Business networks—Juvenile literature. 2. Vocational guidance—Juvenile literature. I. Title.
HD69.S8R69 2008
650.1'3—dc22

                                                    2007034841

Manufactured in the United States of America

contents

As a high school student, you have spent your time perfecting your reading and writing skills, your proficiency in mathematics and science, and your knowledge of U.S. and world history. As your teachers have no doubt told you, this information is essential when making it in the "real world." The knowledge you gain in school will give you the skills you need to start down the road to a long-term career, no matter what you choose to be after you graduate.

However, some skills that are essential to your future success are not usually discussed in high school. Of course, you need to know how to write a business letter and a resume.

You may also need to understand how to calculate percentages and divide fractions. But these are just the foundation skills that will enable you to build the career of your dreams.

Most of us are not taught in school how to talk to coworkers, bosses, and clients. Likewise, schools seldom teach students how to make and keep beneficial contacts when starting down a career path. These are skills we need to cultivate while on the job. If these things aren't taught in school, how can we learn to use them well?

The Work Readiness series is designed to help bridge the gap between graduation and a career. These books discuss important issues that are usually not covered in math class or during English composition. These books will help you to apply the skills you learn in high school to real-world, business-oriented situations. Whether you want to become a physical trainer, a doctor, a cook, or a musician, the books in this series will guide you down the path to success.

What Is a Network? What Is Networking?

"Work readiness" can mean many things. Some of the books in this series will help you to become a better decision maker, while others will focus on communication skills. This book will help you understand the importance of networking. A network is a system of interconnected people. As a member of a network, you can benefit from the things that other members of the network can do for you—particularly the things that help to further your career. Equally important, you will be called upon to help others, too.

Networking is the process of making and maintaining connections. These connections can help you in many ways. You may think "connections" means business connections, but that is not the only meaning of the word. In fact, whenever you talk to someone during the day—whether that person is your parent, a friend, a store clerk, or a police officer—you are networking. In short, anyone you speak to is a potential network connection.

Let's say you bump into an old friend and decide to meet for a cup of coffee—you are networking. You go to your school guidance counselor with a question about career options—you are networking. You attend a town meeting and introduce yourself to a town official—you are networking. In other words, any conversation you have with another person is a chance for you to form an important network connection. You just need to know how to make the most of that connection. In this book, we will see how to recognize opportunities to form networks, how to nurture them, and how to use them to strengthen your career.

chapter one

NETWORKS AND NETWORKING

You might not realize it, but you are already a part of at least one network: your friends and family. These people can be a great help when finding employment, especially if you have no experience in searching for and landing a job.

Family and Friends: A Network in Action

Here's an example of how a family-and-friends network can be helpful in achieving goals. Clark is graduating from high school in a month. He has done very well in science and math, and he even had the chance to attend a vocational school in his final year, learning basic electrician skills. Clark is not sure what he wants to do with these skills after he graduates, and he doesn't think college is the right path for him. Clark's dad tells him to go talk to his cousin Blair, who manages a local electronics shop. Blair tells Clark that she started as a clerk just two years ago and worked her way up to management. She is using the salary to help pay for college. Blair tells Clark that she will recommend him

Your family is a ready-made network that you can count on to help you reach your goals.

for the next opening at the store. Clark fills out an application before leaving.

In the meantime, Clark keeps mowing lawns in his neighborhood, something he has been doing for more than three years. He earns $20 a lawn, which gives him enough spending money for the weekend. However, Clark knows he doesn't want to mow lawns forever. On Thursdays, Clark mows Mr. MacReady's lawn. Mr. MacReady informs Clark that he can get him a job interview with a friend of his who owns a movie rental store.

A few weeks later, Clark interviews for both jobs. He makes a good impression on both employers and is offered both jobs. Clark decides to take the job in the electronics shop; he figures it will best help him to decide how he wants to use the skills he learned in vocational school. Now that Clark has taken the job, however, there is no one to mow Mr. MacReady's lawn. To return the kindness Mr. MacReady showed him, Clark recommends that he hire his friend Garry.

Clark made good use of his network of friends and family to increase his chances of finding a job. Garry and Mr. MacReady also benefited from having Clark in their networks. Not all stories end up like Clark's. Finding a job can be difficult and even frustrating at times. However, Clark's story shows us that being aware of the networks you are already a part of can make the process less difficult. Clark also learned the importance of gaining new network connections. Most networks are made up of people who share the desire to succeed and improve their lives. Let's take a closer look at networks to

People you meet at your house of worship or in other social settings may be able to introduce you to others who can open doors of opportunity.

better understand what it is that makes them so valuable when planning a career.

Growing a Network

Networking is an important component of just about every business or profession. As Clark's example showed us, however, networks do not always involve work or business associates. We are all part of one or more networks that develop naturally the longer we know people and the more people we meet. Family and friends are the easiest type of network to develop. However, we also build networking relationships with people we meet at houses of worship, while playing sports, in the community, and even online. Networking is the way people take advantage of the connections they share.

Growing a network requires effort and organization. You can't simply make a new friend and wait for him or her to offer you a job. You need to be persistent in reminding people of your connection. You also need to be able to recognize an opportunity when one pops up and be bold enough to act on that opportunity before it slips away.

When networking, you will rely on the communication skills you are learning in school. Good writing skills are essential. You will need to write business letters, thank-you letters, summaries, notes, and so on. Good speaking skills are just as essential. You need to be able to make a positive impression on people when talking in person, on the phone, and even through e-mail.

Those who know how to use today's communications technology have an advantage over those who do not. In our digital age, it is important to understand the Internet and e-mail, and office machinery such as photocopiers and fax machines. Not being able to use them will make it more difficult to build and maintain a network.

Networking is a lifelong process. As our networks grow over time, so does our quality of life. Learning to make the most of your acquaintances will enable you to accomplish more and go further. A strong network does not appear overnight. It requires time to develop relationships with people and act on leads. It also requires clear goals and realistic planning. The harder you work

Throughout your life, different social situations will bring you together with a wide range of people. Each one is a potential network contact.

at networking, the easier it will get, and the better you will get at it.

Why Network?

Networking is building a bank of reliable people and resources that can make your life easier, more fulfilling, and more productive. Your network can provide you with options when a problem arises or when you decide to take your career to the next level. Having many strong network connections increases your chances of

10 Great Questions to Ask

1. How do I start a network?

2. Who might already be a part of my network?

3. Where are the best places to network locally?

4. How can I use my network to establish a career?

5. Can my network help me get into the college I want to attend?

6. Where should I start looking for network contacts?

7. What are the best books to read when preparing to network?

8. What Web sites are helpful when networking?

9. How can I find out about local job fairs?

10. Where can I get help writing a resume?

succeeding in your career and in life. Your network connections may become your closest friends.

You may pride yourself on being hardworking and independent, but you can't do everything yourself. A well-tended network can help you achieve your goals in countless ways. Your network may certainly help you get a job. But it might also help you design and put up a Web site for a low price, find that rare baseball card you've been looking for, or find someone to watch your house when you and your family are on vacation. Or you might just get someone smart to talk to when you need advice.

Whether you want to be a mechanic, a botanist, a carpenter, or a teacher, a network can be a guiding force in your professional career. Getting a job after you graduate can sound like a difficult process, but it doesn't have to be. Use your networking skills to make the job search more productive. Make a point of meeting new people and using already established contacts, and you'll open doors you never knew were there.

Networking Is Not "Getting Things"

Networking is not about getting a job, or getting a grant, or getting anything. The major benefit of networking is the network itself. Basically, networking is meeting a person and forming a connection that may someday benefit both of you. It is about sharing information, knowledge, and other contacts. A contact is someone you befriend before you even need his or her help. Most network contacts are mutually beneficial—that is, both individuals can gain something from the friendship.

Maintaining connections is a key to effective networking. Then, when opportunities arise, good networkers are ready to take advantage of them.

Networking is all about making smart contacts and knowing that they may help you someday.

The bigger your network, the greater the chance of getting what you want when you really need it. Just don't forget that you have to be willing to give a favor before you get a favor. Networking is a two-way street.

chapter two

PREPARING TO NETWORK

Building a network is hard if you lack basic communication skills. You may already speak and write very well, since you have probably covered these topics in school. In addition, knowledge of how to use computers, e-mail, and the Internet will also greatly aid your search for network connections. You might consider these things the necessary "tools" of networking. This chapter highlights several skills and tools that will help make networking more productive. Many of the topics mentioned in this chapter are discussed more thoroughly in the other books in the Work Readiness series.

Conversational Skills

Before you can reap the benefits of networking, you need to talk to others and build friendships. Getting practice talking and listening to others—face-to-face—is the best way to develop good conversational skills. This section offers some tips to help you initiate a good conversation with someone you'd like to add to your network.

A confident handshake is one of the best ways to make a good impression on someone you have just met. Don't forget to smile and make eye contact.

First Impressions

First impressions are important. Most people form an opinion about you within ten seconds. A firm handshake is the best way to begin a friendship for both men and women. Eye contact is important. Frequently ask yourself what color the other person's eyes are. Be aware of how you are standing and where your hands are. Slouching and shoving your hands in your pockets can make you seem shy or annoyed. Shifting from foot to foot or gesturing with your hands can make you seem anxious or nervous. Speak clearly when introducing yourself, and don't forget to smile. When someone asks you a question, try to answer with more than just a few words.

Getting to Know You

When first meeting someone, always keep the conversation simple, and speak in a manner the listener will understand. You don't need to cover every topic—just a few interesting and memorable ones. Never start a conversation by stating what it is you hope to get from the other person. Instead, introduce yourself and try to find a topic that both of you will enjoy discussing.

A conversation requires talking and listening. It is good to talk about yourself, but it is bad to dominate a conversation. When you ask a question, wait for the answer. Don't talk over the other person, finish another speaker's sentence, or interrupt. A good rule is to wait three seconds after someone has finished speaking before responding.

Don't just listen passively; be an active participant in the conversation. Active listeners nod to show agreement without interrupting the speaker. They do not play with pens or papers while someone else is talking. They pay attention not only to the speaker's words but also to body language, which sometimes reveals more than words do. Active listeners reflect back what they have heard to get confirmation that they have understood the speaker correctly.

Remain objective. Stay focused on the speaker and hear him or her out, rather than allowing your emotions

People pay attention to body language. This young man is making good eye contact with a college recruiter, but standing with his hands in his pockets makes him appear a little nervous.

to take over. Take time to observe and analyze what the speaker is saying. This will ultimately help you to interact with the speaker in a manner that is beneficial to you both.

What Not to Say

It is a good idea to relate something personal about yourself when meeting someone new. But it is not a good idea to get too personal or to dominate the conversation with your personal stories. It's not always the case, but

When you first meet someone, steer the conversation away from topics that are too serious or heavy. You want the other person to remember how pleasant it was meeting you.

be aware that topics like sports, the weather, and local events may come off as dull or predictable. It is often better to begin a conversation by asking a question and giving the other person a chance to talk. This shows that you are interested in him or her and helps build an immediate connection.

Without fully knowing a person, it is impossible to tell what he or she might find uninteresting or even offensive. After two or three conversations, you will be better able to decide which topics are OK to discuss and which are off-limits. For example, many people disagree on religious topics, and it is usually best to avoid them on a first meeting. On the other hand, if you meet someone at your church, temple, or mosque, or on a religious retreat, talking about religious topics may be the best way to get to know the person.

Writing Skills

When building a successful career, writing skills are usually just as important as conversational skills. Persuasive writing can be a powerful asset. On the other hand, frequent grammatical and spelling errors will convince a potential employer or network contact that you are not worth doing business with. E-mail is less formal than other means of writing, but even e-mails with frequent mistakes will cause someone to think twice about working with you.

Send Me a Letter

The term "business letter" is a catchall for a letter written to achieve a wide variety of results. The contents of a business letter vary depending on the letter's purpose. A well-written business letter can help you get a meeting with someone you've been unable to get on the phone. It could also convince a potential business partner to work with you. Appropriate follow-up letters remind employers that you are eager and capable, and they help you to stand out in a crowd.

Despite the numerous uses for business letters, there are relatively few accepted forms. Businesses and

Parts of a Typical Business Letter

Your Name, Address, and Contact Information

Jonathan Doe
1234 Main Street
Springfield, New York 12345
(617) 555-1234
jdoe@mailserver.com

Date

January 1, 2008

Inside Address

Ms. Emily A. Smith
Chief Executive Officer
Networking Professionals
123 Easy Street
San Diego, California

Salutation

Body Text

Dear Ms. Smith,

This is the first line of the first paragraph. It should state the purpose of the letter or the reason for writing. Be brief and clear. This may be the only paragraph that gets read, so write and rewrite until you have the perfect opening paragraph.

This is the second paragraph. Most business letters have more than one paragraph. Your letter should be more exciting to read than this one, but you should not be too original or casual. Business letters will not be well received unless they have all the necessary elements: heading, date, inside address, salutation, body or text, complimentary closing, your handwritten signature, and your name typed below your signature.

Depending on your purpose, your business letter may have additional elements or may refer to other documents enclosed in the same envelope. Your networking abilities will be greatly enhanced when you learn how to write a standard business letter like this one.

Thank you for considering these tips.

Complimentary Closing

Sincerely,

Jonathan Doe **Signature**
Jonathan Doe

Typed Name

businesspeople usually expect a letter to be formatted in one of several similar ways. Each style has basic elements in common, such as addresses, body text, and signatures. All business letters should be written with a businesslike tone. This is true whether the letter is meant to be a simple reminder of a meeting or a warning about pending legal action.

While they usually look the same, business letters may sound very different depending on their intent. They may also contain different types of information. A letter of application will sound different than the cover letter of a resume. Be careful to write a letter appropriate for its purpose.

Resumes

A resume, sometimes called a CV (short for "curriculum vitae"), is a standard part of any application for employment. All high school graduates should know how to write a solid resume. You might think you don't have enough experience to create one, but all it really takes is one or two previous jobs and a high school education. Resumes are a place to record this information in bite-sized chunks for potential employers to get a better understanding of your employment and educational histories. In addition, resumes often include a summary of your knowledge base and career aspirations.

The purpose of a resume is to get an interview. Essentially, the resume is your first contact with an employer. As such, it needs to be well written and professionally composed. Your resume will evolve and change over time, but it should always follow a clean,

Networking Tools

The following is a list of tools that many networkers use. Some may prove to be more valuable to you than others. Some may be no use at all, depending on the career path you choose.

- Notebooks, journals, notepads
- Pens, highlighters, markers
- Index cards
- Poster board (for brainstorming and mapping your network)
- Address book, date book
- Business cards, card case
- File container for collected business cards
- Thank-you cards
- Phone directories (of schools, companies, nonprofit groups, etc.)
- Briefcase
- Cell phone/PDA
- Computer/laptop
- Printer and printer paper
- Computer software (especially word processing and spreadsheet programs)

structured format. To learn more about writing business letters and resumes, see the references listed in the For More Information section on page 58 in the back of this book.

Stay Organized

Once you begin networking, you need to keep your information organized. If you fail to do so, you may lose

Laptop computers allow people to access network information wherever they go. However, some prefer to keep their networking information written in a notebook.

an important phone number or meeting time, or even a contact's name. All networkers should make good use of networking tools to develop efficient networking methods.

Computers and computer software are invaluable networking tools. Some networkers prefer to keep hand-written notes, but spreadsheets and typed documents can help keep things more organized and easier to recall. Many networkers prefer to keep a journal. They write down important (and not so important) information they can't afford to forget. Perhaps you make a connection who is sure to recommend you for an opening when it comes along. Make sure you write down this person's name, title, phone number, and other contact information. Some prefer to use personal data assistants (PDAs). In the end, it doesn't matter how you keep track of your network, as long as your method is neat and orderly.

chapter three

MAKING CONNECTIONS

Networking is all about people you know. Chances are the more network contacts you have, the further you will get in your career. However, the network with the most people isn't necessarily the strongest network. The key is finding people who can supply exactly what you need to get ahead. In this chapter, we will take a look at the different types of people who may already be in your network and where to meet new ones.

Family and Friends

As mentioned in chapter 1, family and friends are your closest network connections. Parents, best friends, aunts and uncles, and grandparents often help us get our first jobs while we are in high school or right after graduation. The following example will help to illustrate the importance of family and friends.

Sara has just graduated high school. She has been filling out applications around town but hasn't found a job yet. Sara's mother, Ellen, works for a local flower shop. Ellen asks her boss, Caroline, if there is anything

Parents are among your most valuable network connections. They often help you make your first professional decisions by pointing you in the right direction.

Sara can do around the shop to earn some money. Caroline mentions that one of her flower suppliers has been looking for a new employee. Sara goes to apply for the job at the greenhouse right away. The owner, Winston, says that Caroline recommended her for the position. After a short interview, Sara gets the job!

In this example, Ellen did not actually get her daughter the greenhouse job. However, Ellen did prove to be a valuable network connection. Through Ellen, Sara earned two new connections—Caroline, who recommended her for the greenhouse job, and Winston, who ultimately hired her. It is important to note that this is how all networks function, not just family-and-friends networks. It is a game of give and take with the people you know, as well as the people they know.

Academic Connections

The relationships we form with teachers, coaches, and principals are not usually the same as those we share with friends and family. It is often difficult for them to give individual students attention. Still, teachers and coaches typically want to help young people succeed in life. Teachers may be happy to give you advice about colleges or jobs. They may even have connections with people in a career that interests you. Coaches may also be able to give you advice or put you in contact with an employer.

Schools have professional network connections on staff all the time. School guidance counselors can help you prepare for college or employment, as well as for other events. They can also help you to build your network by pointing you in the right directions. Guidance counselors can tell you about job fairs, college tours, employment agencies, military recruiters, and more.

Academic networking can extend beyond high school. If you decide to attend college, you will meet more people who will make great network connections: professors, instructors, resident assistants, coaches, academic advisers, other students, military recruiters, and so on. You may also take continuing education courses once you have graduated high school. There,

Athletic coaches, like teachers and counselors, are usually eager to help young people achieve success in their lives and careers.

too, you will have opportunities to meet plenty of people who are potential network contacts.

What Is a Mentor?

Mentors watch over the progress of less experienced people and foster their development. Mentors are often older than the people they help, but that is not always the case. They don't have to be older than you—just more experienced. Business mentors are people who share their time, knowledge, and experience specifically with someone who is just starting down a similar career path.

You might find a mentor in your family, at school, at your house of worship, or on a sports team. Many people consider their parents mentors. You may also meet one at work as you begin to establish a career. Many businesses and associations have a mentor program to help train young or new employees. You may even be required to mentor a less experienced employee once you are trained. Being asked to mentor someone is an honor.

It is not a given that you will someday have a mentor. As with all endeavors in life, you can rely on others for support, but you should be prepared to grapple with problems on your own. In any case, a mentor— should you be fortunate enough to find one—can be a powerful network ally.

Who Else Is in My Network?

While the types of networks mentioned here are probably the most common, they represent just a handful of the types of people involved in social networking. Virtually everywhere you go during the day has potential as a networking location: the store, your job, your house of worship, even the park. Below is a short list of locations and events that you may already be a part of. The people you see there may become your greatest network contacts.

- Book circles and clubs
- Religious functions
- Town hall
- Libraries
- Neighborhood centers
- Volunteer centers
- Town parks/pools
- Community sports teams
- Musical, dance, or theater groups
- Restaurants/buffets

Expanding Your Network

Now that you have a better idea of who is in your network, you need to consider ways of branching out and finding new network connections. There are many ways to meet new people who share your interests and desire to expand your networking sphere.

Socialize!

One of the most effective and natural ways of expanding your network is to continue doing what you have been doing—socializing. Social networks include members of your house of worship, teammates, coworkers, and fellow volunteers. Anytime you meet and converse with people, you increase the potential of establishing a network connection. Always try to meet at least three new people every time you attend a social function. Chances are at least one of them will prove to be helpful to you in some way.

Clubs, Organizations, and Associations

Joining a club, organization, or association can be a great way to meet new network contacts. Everyone has an interest, hobby, or pastime. Whatever you like to call it, just about every activity has an organization or association dedicated to people who enjoy it. There are business associations, sports organizations, men's and women's clubs, even associations for dog lovers. Many people with whom you share a common interest will be just as happy to add you to their network as you will be to add them to yours.

Networking Groups

Many serious networkers are members of one or more networking groups. These groups meet at regular intervals to talk and exchange information and leads. This might occur once a week, once a month, or a few times a year. The makeup and rules of network groups vary. Some groups are for people from the same industry. Others allow only one person from a given industry or job position at a time to avoid conflicts between two members vying for the same leads and referrals. Some groups have no restrictions on membership. Most net-

A young woman looking to get ahead would be wise to join a women's business group. The group shown above meets regularly at a community college to discuss business opportunities.

work groups require members to pay fees. Fees help guarantee that a member will not back out, and they help to pay for meeting costs, learning materials, and guest speakers.

The more frequently network groups meet, the stronger their network connections grow. If you can afford to join one, the benefits are sure to outweigh the membership fees. Keep in mind that group networkers are usually very serious about the meeting. You will be

The Ups and Downs of Online Networking

Among its many marvels, the Internet has brought everyone in the world closer. Twenty years ago, it was difficult for most people to converse or network with people in distant locations. Today, we can network with people on the other side of the world without leaving our homes!

There are downsides to online networking. For instance, you don't usually see the person with whom you are communicating. This allows many people to be dishonest, making the information you receive from them dubious at best.

Despite the drawbacks, online networking can produce new contacts. While a face-to-face meeting is always best when networking, online networking can help save time and travel expenses. Many Web sites cater to networkers, making it easy and safe to make connections. You might even be able to establish a network contact simply by getting in touch with board members and employees whose names and e-mail addresses appear on the company Web site. For more information on online networking, turn to the section in the back of this book titled For More Information (page 58).

Being aware of the drawbacks of communicating via the Internet can improve your online networking.

expected to contribute to discussions and share leads when appropriate.

Other Options

The business world is a busy place with many opportunities to meet new people and form new connections. If you've ever been to a job fair, you know that you will find many employers and many people looking for jobs. Everyone you meet there is a potential network contact. Plus, it is easy to find people with the same interests at a job fair. Some companies employ headhunters—human resource employees who search for the best person for a position. Headhunters are always excellent additions to your network. You often have to pay for their service, but it is usually worth it.

Although you would probably like to think of it as your last choice, you can also network and find employment at the unemployment office. Unemployment offices are connected to statewide databases filled with leads and job offers. Most also have career counselors and job training classes. These outlets offer you a place to go and look for a job, but they also offer you a chance to strengthen your network.

SUCCESSFUL NETWORKING

O nce you identify your potential network connections, it is time for you to put those connections to the test. Simply developing a network is not enough. You need to discover the ways in which your network can best help you achieve your goals. This takes planning and strategizing.

Strategize

The ability to think quickly and make decisions on the fly is a valuable skill. However, it is always best to plan ahead if you have the time. A well-thought-out strategy will keep you focused on your goals in networking, in your career, and in life. In her book *Networking for Everyone*, L. Michelle Tullier says: "Like any endeavor in life, it's important to have a plan when you are preparing to network. Otherwise, there's no telling where you'll end up or how long it will take to get there."

Whether you are attending a convention, going on a sales call, requesting funding, or simply going to lunch with other people in your network, it is a good idea to

Taking the time to strategize will give you a better idea of what it is you want to do and the best way to go about getting what you want.

prepare what you want to do and say. You may have several days or a week to plan for a meeting with someone. Then again, you may have just five minutes before you need to make a pitch to someone on the telephone. Either way, having a strategy in place will make for better networking.

What Do I Want?

In all of our endeavors, goals serve as signposts of the things we want to achieve. Keeping these signposts in front of us as we work toward them keeps us motivated and focused on the results of our efforts. Our goals reflect who we are and what we want to achieve.

Having clear goals makes it more likely that your network will produce positive results. They can be short-term goals ("Introduce myself to Fred Lewis at the next town meeting and get his phone number"). Or they can be long-term goals ("Get the permits and funding needed to open a bookstore in town"). Either way, we need to look at the size and scope of our goals and make sure they are possible. Our goals need to be ambitious but realistic. Be aware that your goals may change over time. When this happens, you need to reassess what you want to accomplish and then revise your goals accordingly.

What Are My Objectives?

Goals are a picture of the future as we hope it will be. Our goals, especially long-term goals, may sometimes seem out of reach. However, it is important to remember that goals don't just happen—we need to work at them

Write down your goals and objectives as you plan your strategy. You can always make adjustments later if your plans must change.

one step at a time. We can accomplish our goals by setting objectives. Objectives are smaller goals we accomplish on our way to achieving our main goals. If goals are signposts, then objectives can be thought of as mile markers.

As with goals, objectives must be carefully planned when strategizing. Let's say that your goal is to become a world-famous rock star. That's a great goal, but it might be nothing more than a pipe dream if you don't plan out the objectives needed to reach that goal. These objectives would include the following: learn to play an instrument well, find other musicians to start a band, rent studio time, put out a CD, get a manager/agent, and so on. In this way, all of our goals can be broken down into smaller goals called objectives.

How Am I Going to Do It?

Once you have mapped out your goals and objectives, it is time to make a plan for how you will go about achieving them. Ask yourself what you need to do to reach your objectives. The activities that you come up with will become part of your plan. This may include researching a topic at the library. It will also include networking with people who can help you reach your goals.

Goals and objectives represent the big picture. They state what it is you hope to achieve and the steps required to get there. Plans, however, need to be more detailed. Your plan is a list of actions that will help make your goals reality. When recording plans, try to establish exact dates and specific contacts, and then stick to them. Create a plan that is both interesting to you and capable of producing results. Think about what you can do by yourself, as well as whom you can turn to for help and guidance along the way. Ideally, your plan will also enable you to meet many new people, some of whom will turn out to be valuable network contacts.

Sometimes, plans can be overly ambitious or they may be misguided. By doing a little research, you can be sure your plans will be appropriate. Before jotting down an idea for a plan, make sure it is doable by researching the possible methods and outcomes. Once you are sure your plans are practical and possible, record them in your plan. Then it's time to act.

Selling Yourself

When networking, it is in your best interest to present yourself as a competent, motivated individual. You need to convince others that you are worth their time and that you have something to contribute to the relationship. To properly "sell" yourself to potential employers and network connections, you first need to know what it is you want and how you plan to get it. You can do this by

A Road Map for Success

Howard is training to become a world-class competitive eater. He realizes that he needs to create a plan of his goals and objectives. Howard sits down and writes out his strategy.

Goal: Become a world champion competitive eater.
  Objective 1: Improve my eating techniques.
  Plan A: Watch video footage of past champions during competitions.
  Plan B: Practice with the foods generally used in food competitions.
  Plan C: Attend competitive eating competition at Coney Island and meet at least three new people.
  Plan D: Attend lecture by champion eater Takeru Kobayashi in May. Try to get face time with Kobayashi and other competitive eaters in attendance.

  Objective 2: Increase the amount of food I can eat in one sitting.
  Plan A: Purchase stretchy pants for practice and competitions.
  Plan B: Conduct scientific research at the library and online to find out more about how the body digests food, particularly hot dogs, chicken wings, pasta, and pie.
  Plan C: Dine in at least one local restaurant per week. Strive to meet owners and managers who might want to become sponsors to fund my training and travel expenses.
  Plan D: Get acquainted with local grocery store managers and workers who may be able to give me a discount on certain food items.

Notice that his goal is broken down into objectives, and his objectives are broken down into actions, or plans.

People in your network may have already found success doing what you hope to do one day. Meeting with one of these people can lead to a more effective strategy.

strategizing, as discussed in the previous sections. You can also speak with people about your interests and aspirations, write a resume, or keep a journal of your thoughts. Activities like these will help you understand your strengths, goals, interests, and personality. In turn, you will develop the confidence necessary to do well in an interview or make a new network connection.

Once you have a strong grasp of who you are and what you have to offer, then you can begin to sell yourself to others. Although network relationships are a two-way street, you will need to talk a fair amount about yourself for the other people to understand why they would want you in their networks. Don't be afraid to tell others about your aspirations and strengths. These details will help get you noticed, which is important when strengthening and extending your network.

Take Advantage of Opportunities

You should always be ready to take advantage of new networking opportunities—planned and unplanned. When you are attending a social event or business gathering, make it a priority to meet at least three new people. Chances are at least one of those people will be able to help you build your network. By frequently meeting new people, you improve your conversational skills and increase your network. This will increase your chances of achieving the goals you have set up.

After you have met a new network contact, don't neglect him or her. Even if there is nothing the person can do for you right now, keep the lines of communication open. You may establish a valuable friendship with this person simply by speaking with him or her over the phone. Then again, there might be something you can do for the other person, which will strengthen your connection. It's always nice having people in your network who "owe you one"!

It's common for people in your network to offer you a lead. This is the name or number of someone who might be able to help you. When you are given a lead, promptly contact that person. And when you are contacted by a referral, be ready to take advantage of the situation. Don't allow these types of opportunities to

A potential employer is more likely to hire you when you speak well, act professionally, and show proper respect.

slip away—they are exactly the reason why you are networking in the first place. Likewise, never forget to follow up with people whom you have already contacted. Be on time for meetings, and send a thank-you letter after meeting with an important person. While you don't want to pester or annoy a potential network contact, you certainly don't want that person to forget about you.

chapter five

NETWORKING ON THE JOB

Thanks to your diligent networking, you were able to get a job and start your career. Congratulations! Now you can throw out all those networking notes and contacts. You have the job you were hoping for, so you no longer need to network, right?

Wrong. Networking is not just about finding a job. It is not about getting things, or making money. It is about establishing and maintaining a system of friends and acquaintances that will help you succeed in your career—and in many other parts of your life. Getting a job is a big step in the right direction, but it is just one step. Continuously maintaining and strengthening your network will benefit you for the rest of your life.

Maintaining Your Network

Once you have formed a network, it is important to maintain connections. Even after you have a job, it is a good idea to keep your network alive and well. How do you tend to your network, even if you aren't actively relying on your contacts as resources?

Sending an e-mail is a great way to maintain network connections. It's faster than regular mail, and it makes more sense than giving a phone call when you don't have much to say.

While some may disagree, it is sometimes prudent to reward network contacts who helped you find employment. Gift giving is a common practice among networking professionals. It doesn't have to be something expensive. It could be as simple as a bouquet of flowers or a gift card to a local coffee shop. Again, the size and cost of the gift is not important. What is important is that you show gratitude to a helpful network contact. A small gift will make you more memorable and will strengthen your networking relationship.

Call network contacts from time to time, even just to say hello and find out what's new. Volunteer your help any way you can. When people call you for advice or a favor, it is in your best interest to do what you can for them. Returning the favor is a great way to guarantee that people in your network will be there for you next time you need them. Some contacts you will end up seeing on a regular basis, which will make it easier for you to help each other.

Much of our discussion so far has focused on increasing the number of network contacts you have. As you mature in your role as a networker, however, you may start to be a bit more discerning about whom you include in your network. Luckily, there are a lot of dedicated businesspeople out there who are serious about their networks. You can never have too many of these people in your network. However, you will come to realize that not all people make good network connections. You may run into a few people who are not interested in the give-and-take aspects of networking. These types do everything for themselves. They may accept a favor from you one day and refuse to return it the next. In time, you'll figure out how to distinguish the few selfish networkers from the majority of sharing networkers.

Business Networking

Once you have a job, the network connections that you have up to that point will still be of value to you. Then, as you work at your job, you will begin to add a whole new layer of network contacts to your list. The longer

The relationships you build with coworkers can be valuable when establishing a career. Knowing a lot of people in your chosen field increases your opportunities.

you are at your job, the more people you meet, and the more contacts you will be able to add to your network. These might include coworkers, managers, clients, and so on. It may also include people who visit your place of work occasionally, such as couriers and other service providers. Most business contacts are sure to help you out in a time of need, especially when they work with you on a frequent basis.

You may find yourself in a job one day where networking is just as important as other skills. Salespeople who work on commission, for example, usually spend as much time networking as they do selling. When not making a sale, they are making connections with people, which will increase the chances that they will make a sale in the future. The connections you make with other businesspeople may benefit you for the length of your career, or longer.

Leaving a Job

Just because you have found a job and are working on your career doesn't mean that you will be in that position for the rest of your life. Some people begin working for a company or organization and decide to stay with it for the long haul. Perhaps they get promoted and receive raises on a regular basis and can't see the point in searching for a new job. However, other people feel the need to move to another company or even a new line of work. This is common when a worker is bored or in search of a better salary, or when a company is laying off personnel.

Once you have determined what career path you want to follow, you tend to meet and befriend the types of people who can help you as you travel that path. These are people who can get you interviews with new companies or let you know when they will be hiring. For example, Alicia takes photographs of children and families for a local department store. She likes her job, but she thinks she could make more money and have more fun working elsewhere. Alicia decides to do some networking. She calls an art teacher who used to be her instructor to ask for tips on searching for photography jobs. She calls a friend to help her write a resume. Last, she calls a former

It always works to your advantage to be sociable yet professional with your coworkers and bosses—even after leaving a job.

employer who now works for a major U.S. newspaper. Alicia is making good use of her network to further her career. Simply knowing someone doesn't guarantee you will get a job based on a recommendation. However, network connections often help get your foot in the door.

Let's say that your networking was successful, and you find a better job. Even when leaving a company, it is wise to do so in a professional manner. Remaining on good terms with former bosses, managers, and coworkers will guarantee that many of them will remain in your network in the future. On the other hand, "burning bridges" before leaving for your new job will certainly reduce the number of people in your network. Always give two weeks' notice when leaving a job, and do your best to make the transition a smooth one for everybody. If you are asked to give an exit interview, be as courteous and complimentary as possible. You never know, down the road, you may be able to benefit from the people you are leaving behind.

A Networking Success Story

Ira J. Wood is an operations manager for Hudson Medical Communications, a medical education and communications company. As operations manager, he is responsible for the smooth running of the workplace and facilities. Mr. Wood manages teams of phone operators who serve doctors and health care professionals all across the country. In this interview, he reveals how networking has made a difference for him.

Q. *How has networking helped you get where you are in your career?*

A. *Through a network contact, I learned about a company looking for a telemarketing company to call doctors' offices and provide patient information for their waiting rooms. My company had recently completed a similar project, so I called up the sales director of this company and convinced him to hire us based on our past experience. Because we added a new client, our company was able to reach our end-of-the-year profit goal, and I was promoted to senior manager.*

Q. *As a professional operations manager, how are networking and your network important to you?*

A. *Through networking, I have secured long-term working relationships with the leading service providers in the health care industry. I rely on colleagues in my network to offer their opinions or experience in working with a specific company. Their advice minimizes the amount of time it takes to select and hire a service provider.*

Q. *When someone in your network contacts you with a question or favor, how do you respond?*

A. *I respond as soon as possible with something to offer. In most situations, responding benefits both of us. They get the help they needed, and I know if the favor needs to be returned, I can count of them to respond.*

Q. *What advice would you give someone who is just beginning to network?*

A. *Join professional organizations that meet on a regular basis. Ask friends and family to recommend professionals they know or have worked with. They can even introduce you to key people. Book clubs or volunteering also create opportunities to meet new people. Online associations may offer chat rooms or blogs that can be useful in reaching a wider range of professionals.*

Always have business cards on hand. You never know when you might run into someone who could become an important networking contact. Exchanging business cards is a great way to start a professional relationship.

Networking for Life

Networking is a lifelong process. The more you do it, the better you get at it. You will continue to benefit from your network in many ways, as long as you maintain it. Over time, you will develop the ability to see how people can fit into your network, or if you don't want them in your network at all.

Don't be afraid to jump right in and start networking. Go out and meet three new people today. One of those people might prove to be your greatest network ally.

glossary

application Standard form most employers require when you apply for a job. Most applications ask for basic information, including your work history.

aspiration Desire or ambition to achieve something.

beneficial Helpful; producing desired results.

blog Online journal or newsletter that is periodically updated by the author. Short for "Web log."

colleague Person someone works with.

competent Having the skill or ability to do something well.

cultivate To improve or refine through careful effort.

database Organized collection of information.

diligent Showing a persistent and hardworking effort in doing something.

discerning Discriminating or selective.

headhunter Human resource employee who finds individuals to fill positions.

human resources Field of business concerned with recruiting and managing employees.

interpersonal Regarding the relationships between people.

mutual Having or involving the same feelings toward each other.

objective (adj.) Not clouded by personal feelings or prejudices; (n.) something toward which an effort is directed, such as an aim, goal, or intent.

potential With a possibility of occurring some time in the future.

proficiency Advancement in ability or skill.

referral Someone who does business with you based on the recommendation of a third party.

resume A typed record of someone's educational and employment experience for the information of possible employers.

spreadsheet A chart or table made by a computer program that displays numerical data in rows and columns.

strategize To devise a course of action.

vocational school A school where students are trained in a trade or skill that may be used when pursuing a career.

Association of Professional Communication
    Consultants (APCC)
3924 South Troost
Tulsa, OK 74105
Web site: http://www.consultingsuccess.org
This association refers you to consultants who can help
    with professional writing and communication.

Business Network International (BNI)
545 College Commerce Way
Upland, CA 91786
(800) 825-8286
E-mail: bni@bni.com
Web site: http://www.bni.com
BNI is the "World's Largest Referral Organization."
    Benefits of membership in BNI include newsletters,
    job search systems, networking workshops, and more.

BNI Canada
Web site: http://www.bnicanada.ca
This is the Canadian version of BNI (see above). There
    are more than 250 chapters across Canada. Go to its
    Web site for specific contact information.

Career Planning and Adult Development Network
4965 Sierra Road
San Jose, CA 95132
(408) 559-4946
Web site: http://www.careernetwork.org
An international networking organization that can put
    you in contact with career counselors. The Web site
    offers several useful resources.

Professional Association of Resume Writers & Career
    Coaches (PARW/CC)
1388 Brightwaters Boulevard NE
St. Petersburg, FL 33704
(800) 822-7279
E-mail: PARWhq@aol.com
Web site: http://www.parw.com
People seeking help writing a resume or starting a career
    can find many professional career coaches here.

SearchForEvents.com
P.O. Box 881002
Boca Raton, FL 33488-1002
(800) 672-7959
E-mail: support@searchforevents.com
Web site: http://www.searchforevents.com
An online organization that posts networking opportunities
    in the United States, Canada, and other countries.
    The site also offers resources for networking and
    starting a business.

Web Sites

Due to the changing nature of Internet links, Rosen
Publishing has developed an online list of Web sites
related to the subject of this book. This site is updated
regularly. Please use this link to access the list:

http://www.rosenlinks.com/wr/nesk

Bennie, Bough. *101 Ways to Improve Your Communication Skills Instantly*. San Antonio, TX: GoalMinds, Inc., 2005.

Bond, Alan. *300+ Successful Business Letters for All Occasions*. Hauppauge, NY: Baron's Educational Series, 2005.

Darling, Diane. *The Networking Survival Guide: Get the Success You Want by Tapping into the People You Know*. New York, NY: McGraw-Hill, 2003.

Hansen, Katherine. *Dynamic Cover Letters for New Graduates*. Berkeley, CA: Ten Speed Press, 1998.

Hansen, Katherine. *A Foot in the Door: Networking Your Way into the Hidden Job Market*. Berkeley, CA: Ten Speed Press, 2000.

Lowe, Doug. *Networking for Dummies*. Indianapolis, IN: Wiley Publishing, 2007.

Nierenberg, Andrea. *Nonstop Networking: How to Improve Your Life, Luck, and Career*. Herdon, VA: Capital Books, 2002.

Ryan, Liz. *Happy About Online Networking: The Virtual-ly Simple Way to Build Professional Relationships*. Silicon Valley, CA: Happy About, 2006.

Tullier, L. Michelle. *Networking for Job Search and Career Success*. St. Paul, MN: Jist Publishing, 2004.

Whitcomb, Susan Britton. *Resume Magic: Trade Secrets of a Professional Resume Writer*. St. Paul, MN: Jist Publishing, 2006.

bibliography

Crispin, Gerry, and Mark Mehler. *CareerXroads*. Kendall Park, NJ: MMC Group, 2003.

Darling, Diane. *The Networking Survival Guide: Get the Success You Want by Tapping into the People You Know*. New York, NY: McGraw-Hill, 2003.

Enelow, Wendy S., and Shelly Goldman. *Insider's Guide to Finding a Job*. St. Paul, MN: Jist Publishing, 2005.

Hinds, Josh. "Networking Made Easy." Best Networking Advice. May 17, 2007. Retrieved August 2, 2007 (http://businessnetworkingadvice.com/2007/05/networking-made-easy-by-josh-hinds.html).

Kerr, Cherie. *Networking Skills That Will Get You the Job You Want*. Cincinnati, OH: Betterway Books, 1999.

Kramer, Marc. *Power Networking*. Chicago, IL: VGM Career Horizons, 1998.

Roebke, Nancy. "The Truth About Belonging to Networking Groups." Canadian Women's Business Network. Retrieved August 7, 2007 (http://www.cdnbizwomen.com/articles/netwk4.html).

Tullier, L. Michelle. *Networking for Everyone! Connecting with People for Career and Job Success*. St. Paul, MN: Jist Publishing, 1998.

Tullier, L. Michelle. *Networking for Job Search and Career Success*. St. Paul, MN: Jist Publishing, 2004.

index

A

academic connections, 30–32

B

body language, 18–19
business connections, 49–51
business letters, writing, 4, 11,
22–25

C

clubs/organizations, joining, 34
connections, types of, 6, 28–32,
33–34
conversational skills, 17–22, 45
what not to say, 20–22

E

eye contact, making, 18

F

family and friends, as network,
7–9, 10–11, 28–30
first impressions, 18–19

G

gift giving, and networking, 48
goals, having, 40–42, 43
guidance counselors, as part of
network, 6, 30

H

handshake, having a firm, 18
headhunters, 37

J

job fairs, 37
jobs
leaving, 52–53
networking to find new,
51–52

L

leads, following up on, 45
listening to others, importance
of, 19–20

M

mentors, 32

N

network
definition of, 5
examples of, 10–11, 28–30,
32–33, 37
expanding your, 33–35, 45–46
forming a, 11–12, 14,
28–37, 54
maintaining your, 47–49
networking
definition of, 6, 10, 14–15
importance of, 12–15, 47,
53–54
online, 36
questions to ask about, 13
skills/tools needed for, 11,
17–27
strategizing and, 38–42, 44
networking groups, 34–35

About the Author

Greg Roza is a writer and editor specializing in library books and educational materials. He lives in Hamburg, New York, with his wife, Abigail; his son, Lincoln; and his daughters, Autumn and Daisy. Roza has a master's degree in English from SUNY Fredonia. To this day, he continues to use networking to strengthen his career.

Photo Credits

Cover (top, left to right) © www.istockphoto.com/Stefan Klein, © www.istockphoto.com/dagmar heymans, © www.istockphoto.com/Chris Schmidt; cover (middle, left to right) © www.istockphoto.com; cover (bottom, left to right) © www.istockphoto.com/Jacob Wackerhausen, © www.istockphoto.com/Chris Schmidt, © www.istockphoto.com/Ljupco; pp. 7, 17, 28, 38, 47 (left) © www.istockphoto.com/Stefan Klein, (middle, right) © www.istockphoto.com/Chris Schmidt; p. 8 © Yellow Dog Productions/Taxi/Getty Images; p. 10 © Douglas McFadd/Getty Images; p. 12 © Journal-Courier/Clayton Stalter/The Image Works; p. 15 © www.istockphoto.com/Sean Bolt; p. 18 © www.istockphoto.com/Geoffrey Hammond; p. 20 © Bob Daemmrich/The Image Works; p. 21 © www.istockphoto.com/Nicole S. Young; p. 26 © www.istockphoto.com/automatika; p. 29 © Elizabeth Crews/The Image Works; p. 31 © www.istockphoto.com/Nancy Louie; p. 35 © James Marshall/The Image Works; p. 36 © www.istockphoto.com/Jan van den Brink; p. 39 © Shutterstock.com; p. 41 © www.istockphoto.com/Kyle Nelson; p. 44 © Jeff Greenberg/The Image Works; p. 46 © Alan Carey/The Image Works; p. 48 © www.istockphoto.com/Andrew Manley; p. 50 © Loungepark/Stone/Getty Images; p. 52 © Ryan McVay/Taxi/Getty Images.

Designer: Nelson Sá; **Editor:** Christopher Roberts
Photo Researcher: Marty Levick